«With a saw of gold, the angels hewed twisting hills to make a palace for you». These simple unaffected words from *Virolai*, by Jacint Verdaguer, express the wonder many people feel when contemplating the mountain of Montserrat, moved as they are by a millennium of devotion to the image of Our Lady.

The mountain, a symbol of the presence of the godhead in all religions, at Montserrat has been a place of Christian worship and the site of a Benedictine monastery since the eleventh century.

Mountain, Shrine, Monastery and place of discovery are the core elements that form the complex and surprising world of Montserrat.

MONTSERRAT

Text:
Josep Mª Soler i Canals

Photographs, design, lay-out and printing, entirely
created by the technical department of
EDITORIAL FISA ESCUDO DE ORO, S.A.

Rights of total or partial reproduction and
translation reserved.

Copyright of this edition for photographs and text:
© EDITORIAL FISA ESCUDO DE ORO, S.A.
www.eoro.com

4th Edition

I.S.B.N. 978-84-378-2077-4

Legal Dep. B. 1721-2008

ESCUDO DE ORO

Montserrat

Aerial view of the monastery.

A SURPRISING WORLD

Situated 38 kilometres from Barcelona, near the towns of Manresa and Igualada, the unusual and graceful massif of Montserrat rises in the centre of Catalonia to 1,236 metres above sea level at the highest point, the Pic de Sant Jeroni. The surprising and eye-catching shapes of the mountain came into being through the forces of geological change in the distant past.

At the beginning of the Tertiary period, in the Eocene epoch, a stretch of mountainous land, the so-called Balearic continent, occupied what is now the Mediterranean Sea between the Balearic Isles and the Principality. A large river ran through this area and out into the gulf which occupied the area of what is now the Ebre basin. The slow action of geological disturbances

The apse of the basilica.

4

caused the continent to sink and the deposit of sedimentary material emerged and rose to a significant height because of the depression of the surrounding land. This sedimentary material, consisting of pebbles, bonded together by hard natural limestone cement, sands and clays, formed the mountain of Montserrat. It measures 10 km in length and 5 km in width with an elliptical perimeter of some 25 kms.

The unmistakable appearance of this small mountainous group is the reason why its name, translated into English, is «the serrated mountain». Water, sun, rain, frost and wind have all patiently worked it to create a number of perspectives. The great wealth of vistas it offers has captivated the popular imagination and has inspired numerous writers. Goethe, moved by his friend Humboldt's tale, wrote «man will find rest in no place except his own Montserrat», an expression which was glossed by a Catalan poet when he said «when I am pricked by the thorn of homesickness, I feel Montserrat within me».

The Montserrat which nature presents us is indeed spectacular and already a symbol of introspection, but the true significance of the mountain cannot be fully comprehended unless we consider its close ties with the people who have visited and lived on it over the centuries. The setting for a long and eventful past, Montserrat is tightly bound to the vicissitudes that have affected the Catalan lands and helps us to understand its cultural and religious significance for Catalonia up to the present day. Numerous archeological finds, especially of ceramics decorated with a variety of patterns, provide evidence of human presence on the mountain since the Neolithic

Montserrat

The practically vertical wall of Sant Jeroni *and the unmistakable silhouette of* El Cavall Bernat.

period. This prehistoric culture, which dates back to around 3,000 years BC, is called «Montserratina» because of the specific location and unusual nature of the finds. There are also traces of cultures such as the Bronze and Iron Ages, and the Monastery has pieces of flint, metal objects and human remains from the much later Iberian period. But it would be many years before the Montserrat of history began.

The text of a donation made by Wilfred the Hairy to the Pyrenean Monastery of Ripoll is the first written information we have. Wilfred, the first Count of Barcelona, had conquered the Arabs and taken the land around Montserrat between 875 and 876. Shortly afterwards, in 888, he donated a part of this conquered land with the four hermitages on it to Ripoll. Two of these hermitages, Sant Martí and Sant Per, were

Montserrat, seen from Monistrol.

View from the Sant Miquel *path.*

at the foot of the mountain and two were higher up on the mountain: Santa Maria, the origins of the current Basilica, and Sant Iscle, the only one which still exists today, built in what are now the Monastery gardens probably during the period of the Visigoths before the Arab invasion in 711. Thus began Montserrat's development.

THE MONASTERY IS BORN

The privileged site of the mountain, its steep rock formations and its silence soon attracted Christians, who led a life of prayer and penitence there. However, the flowering of Montserrat began with the fame acquired by the Hermitage of Santa Maria.

Ripoll was an influential centre concerned with other matters and scarcely paid any attention to its small distant churches on Montserrat. So, in the middle of the tenth century, the abbot of the Monastery of Santa Cecília, located on the mountain itself, claimed the property for himself until such time as it was reclaimed from him before the civil and religious authorities.

In 1008, Oliba, son of the count of Besalú and Cerdanya, Oliba Cabreta, and great-grandson of Wilfred the Hairy, was elected as abbot of Ripoll. He recommended the dispute over the possession of the hermitages and surrounding lands on Montserrat and won them back for his Monastery. Oliba was one of the most important figures in Romanesque Catalonia. He was an advocate of the arts and literature and a careful writer, and turned Ripoll into an important religious and cultural centre. He was soon elected as abbot of Sant Miquel de Cuixà and shortly after

Montserrat

Montserrat is surrounded by towns and villages.

that was named bishop of Vic. It was he who instituted the Treva de Déu *(the Peace of God),* which limits the length of struggles and combats. Once the hermitages on Montserrat had been regained, Oliba decided to establish a new monastery on the solitary mountain and installed a group of monks from Ripoll in the hermitage of Santa Maria. This was in 1025. The small Benedictine monastic community soon received visitors and pilgrims, who began to spread stories of the miracles and wonders worked there by Our Lady. These tales of extraordinary healings and grace, so much to the taste of the Middle Ages, brought increasing numbers of pilgrims and donations to the nascent priory. It soon became clear that the old chapel was too small and in the twelfth century a new one had to be built. The façade of this Romanesque chapel still remains in one of the side walls of the Basilica atrium.

The six «Canticles» dedicated by King Alphonse the Wise to Saint Mary of Montserrat are evidence of her growing fame and tell of many wonders and give thanks to Our Lady.

Mui grandes noit'e dia
devemos dar porende
nos a Sancte Maria
graças, porque defende
os seus de dano
et sen engano
en salvo os guia.

(Full many a long night and day we must give thanks to Saint Mary, for she protects us from danger and does not mislead but guides us to safety).

Montserrat

HISTORICAL BACKGROUND

Starting in the thirteenth century, the character of Montserrat become more and more clearly defined. Rapid and vigorous growth has made it the most prestigious Shrine in Catalonia and one of the best-known throughout the Christian world. With the conquests of the Catalan-Aragonese crown, devotion to Our Lady of Montserrat spread eastwards to such an extent that the number of churches and chapels dedicated to her in the Italian regions reached 150. Her cult later spread into central Europe. The fame of Montserrat travelled to the west when the Americas were evangelised because of the early bonds created through the presence of a former monk from the mountain, Bernard Boïl, who was travelling with Christopher Columbus as the Papal Legate. 1409 was to be the most important year for the future of the Monastery; Benedict XIII decided to grant it independence from the abbey at Ripoll and the first abbot of Montserrat elected by the monks was Marc de Vilalba, a man of great diplomatic qualities who actively participated in the politics of the country. One of his successors, Antoni Pere Ferrer, continued this policy and took a strong position against John II in the civil war which started after the death of the prince of Viana.

However, these political struggles had a noticeable effect on the Monastery and made it difficult to lead a monastic life there, and so the need for reform began to be felt. In 1493 Ferdinand II, the Catholic Monarch, annexed Montserrat to the Congregation of San Benito el Real in Vallodolid and this entailed the arrival of

Roca Foradada *and* la Cadireta.

Montserrat

The eye-catching Boleta del Portell Estret.

View of soaring Cavall Bernat.

Castilian monks who did not know the language and customs of the country. In spite of the difficulties caused by the royal imposition of reform (for example, Abbot Joan de Peralta was removed from the Monastery by being named bishop of Vic), the Monastery went through a period of regeneration under the direction of Abbot Garsias de Cisneros, who was first cousin to the famous cardinal of the same name. Cisneros was a deeply religious man and a good organiser. He wrote the «Exercise of Spiritual Life», which was widely circulated and was highly influential on the writings of Ignatius of Loyola, and took effective charge of his monks' monastic and cultural life. In 1499 he brought the new art of printing to the Monastery by taking on the German master Johannes Luschner.

El Sentinella *(The Sentinel), one of the many capricious forms the mountain takes.*

Montserrat

Els Flautats
Roca de Sant Salvador
Cavall Bernat
St. Jeroni
Les Talaies
Ecos
Els Aurons

Pla de la Trinitat
La Mòmia
L'Elefant
Roca de St. Salvador
Els Flautats

Montserrat

Coll de Porc · El Novici · El Frare Gros · El Bastó del Frare · El Lloro · El Bisbe · La Nina · La Boleta Foradada · Agulla del Centenar · El Queixal · El Gendarme · La Boleta del Portell Estret · Coll de les Agulles · L'Escorpí · La Torta · L'Agulla dels Ossos · L'Arbret · La Bandereta

Cavall Bernat · Paret dels Diables · Serrat del Patriarca · Paret del Mirador del Moro · Coll de Porc · Frares

Montserrat

The Sant Jeroni *peak*, La Mòmia *(the mummy)*, La Momieta *(the little mummy) and* La Trompa de l'Elefant *(the elephant's trunk).*

Hermitry, which had existed at Montserrat for many years and in all probability since before the founding of the Monastery, continued to flourish at that time and was to continue until the Napoleonic Wars. The life of work and prayer led by the hermits in their hermitages dotted around the mountains was governed by the Father Superior at the Monastery in accordance with established rules and customs.

The considerable activity at the Shrine clearly demonstrated the small size of the Romanesque church, a problem which was not resolved until Bartomeu Garriga was named abbot and in 1560 began the construction of the current church with loyal support from pilgrims and visitors. The work was finished in 1592.

The seventeenth century was a tumultuous and difficult period for Montserrat because of the wars, which laid the Principality to waste, and because of the heightened tension eventually caused by the new régime introduced by the monks from Valladolid. In 1641, when the uprising against the central authorities took place during the Reapers' War, the most important representative body in Catalonia, the Diputació del Govern General, took the monks imposed by the Castilian crown to the border. However, once the uprising had been quashed, Montserrat once again came under the control of Valladolid.

Montserrat was fortified twice when the French Wars broke out in spite of its poor suitability as a strategic site. In 1811 and 1812 Napoleon's army burnt it down and blew up the group of buildings, leaving the Shrine practically in ruins. The wealth of treasure donated during the previous centuries had been sold by the community to sustain resistance against the invaders. In 1812, only a pile of scorched stones and some half-destroyed buildings remained of the

The Cavall Bernat.

La Mola de Sant Salvador *and the group of* Els Flautats *(the flutes).*

Montserrat

Montserrat

Ruins of the church of Sant Pau Vell.

former Montserrat. Fortunately, the Image of Our Lady was saved as it had been hidden somewhere on the mountain.

During the troubled nineteenth century, Montserrat began the slow process of renewal and reconstruction against the background of the political struggles of the period. However, everything came to a halt with the 1835 Decree of Disentailment and the law on the dissolution of religious orders which meant the community had to leave the Monastery. When the monks returned in 1844, they came back to an enormous task fraught with difficulties and problems. In 1858 the Pope named Miquel Muntades abbot of Montserrat and, as the Congregation at Valladolid had disappeared, the Monastery became fully independent again and adhered to the Italian Congregation of

Subiaco. Efforts to reconstruct the Shrine then increased. This reconstruction was to be very important for the people of Catalonia, closely linked as it was to the Renaixença (Renaissance–the literary, cultural and political rebirth of Catalonia) which made large groups of Catalans aware of their distinctive characteristics. This combination of events brought about the celebration of the supposed 1000th anniversary in 1888 of the founding of the Monastery and, the following year, the festivities surrounding the coronation of the image of Our Lady as patron saint of Catalonia as granted by Pope Leo XIII. In order to help pilgrims visiting the Monastery, the much-loved rack railway was built in 1892 and continued to run until 1957. Finally, during the course of the twentieth century, special mention must be made of Abbot

View of the mountain from el Bruc.

Montserrat

Another view of the massif (Sant Jeroni, 1.235 m).

The cable-car over the River Llobregat.

Antoni M. Marcet, whose leadership brought about intense religious and cultural development within the community, with the establishment of the Monastery library and the First Liturgical Congress held in 1915 (with two further Congresses in 1965 and 1990), which led to a renewal in the liturgy in many areas of the Church in Catalonia. Improvements were also made during this period to the approaches to the Shrine with the installation of cable cars and funiculars.

The 1936 civil war caused little material damage to the Monastery as it had been seized by the government of the Generalitat de Catalunya, although twenty-three monks lost their lives. Once the civil war was over, the image of Our Lady was enthroned on its new throne in 1947, prompted by Abbot Aureli M. Escarré

The cable-car soon reaches the Shrine.

18

The Monastery, built upon a flat shelf on the mountain.

and supported by public contributions. Many people attended the celebrations, which were a popular cultural renewal of Catalonia after the war. Abbot Escarré continued in the direction taken by his predecessor, Abbot Marcet, and encouraged cultural flowering at the Monastery as well as developments in the liturgy and monastic life and physical improvements to the Shrine. His successors, Abbot Gabriel M. Brasó, Abbot Cassià M. Just and the current abbot, Sebastià M. Bardolet, have all continued the same policies while adapting them to new trends and concerns. Recent years have also seen *empts to re-establish the reclusive life of her-
on the mountain.

*atures, which have marked the history
*rat, enable us to understand the
* the Shrine and Monastery have
*. Montserrat is a rich and var-
* at times disconcerting. It
*th its natural or artistic
religious and human
*linked to the feel-
*a.

A group of Benedictine nuns settled in the former Monastery of Santa Cecília in 1952 and moved to the Monastery of Sant Benet in 1955, some four kilometres from the Marian Shrine, where they continue their life of prayer and receive pilgrims.

The two monasteries, the presence of hermits and the pilgrims make the mountain of Montserrat a place of worship and prayer to God, a place for deepening spiritual values and making supplications for the joys and troubles of all humanity.

A LAND OF FANTASY: THE NATURAL PARK

The visual spectacle to be enjoyed in contemplating the mountain cannot be momentary or hurried. We need to be serene in order to be able to absorb all its beauty and to fix our eyes on the unusual rock formations and the harmony of the great wealth of vegetation.

Montserrat grows and transforms itself before our very eyes; it becomes alive, constantly changes colour, takes on new perspectives and its peaks, often surrounded by cloud, seem in our marvelling imagination to fly up to the sky. The shape of the mountain is so astonishing, so improbable, that it is unique throughout the world and might even make us think of the creative hand of an artist or child...

The fantastic shapes of the rocks and needles of Montserrat inspired people living long ago in nearby villages to give names to the most important formations – names as poetic or picturesque as «Els Frares encantats» (the enchanted monks), «El Camell» (the camel), «El Cap de mort» (Death's head), «Els flautats» (the flutes), «La Mòmia» (the mummy), «El Cavall Bernat» (Bernàrd the horse), «La Roca forada» (the pitted rock), «La Cadireta» (the small chair)... These people also wove strange tales around these rocks.

It is still surprising that such a rocky massif as this should have such exuberant vegetation in spite of the devastating fires in recent years. All around trees, bushes and plants cling to the rock itself in their eagerness for invincible life and

Bear's ear (Ramonda myconi).

Bonelli's eagle and goats.

Montserrat

21

The peage bayflower (*Campanula speciosa subsp. affinis*).

Queen's crown (*Saxifraga callosa subsp. catalunica*).

beauty. These plants flourish in the favourable climactic conditions 1000 metres above sea level, in the shady damp ravines, in the sunny wind-blown rocky outcrops which offer rich soil to plant life (holm oaks, yews, pines, rosemary, heather, box trees etc.) and a favourable environment for a wide variety of animals (including wild boar, badgers, weasels, foxes and vipers, as well as the recently re-introduced goats), especially birds (eagles, ravens, owls, woodpigeons, blackbirds, etc.), and a large number of insect varieties.

The interior of the rocks has also been worked by water and other agents. The caves of Salnitre in the area of Collbató were formed in this way. These caves, which are over 500 metres long, offer the visitor an astonishing journey amongst stalactites and stalagmites which are interesting from a scientific point of view and suggestive to the artistic mind. Some of the chasms are over a hundred metres in depth. There are grottoes, some of which were used in prehistoric times for dwellings and burial places, while others became shelters for hermits and there are many others which were the object of various popular stories.

All this wealth and diversity produces a world of wonder, which, between the fable of the enchanted land and the material world of men and women today, lives and breathes in the very heart of Montserrat.

The mountain is a homogenous ensemble, geographically, geologically and geomorphically, which constitutes a special ecological unit within the natural environment of Catalonia with a unique richness, particularly as far as flora are concerned. The Patronat de la Muntanya de Montserrat (the Mountain of Montserrat Association) was founded in 1950 to ensure the conservation of this environment and in 1989, to widen this protection, the Parlament de Catalunya (the Parliament of Catalonia) created the Natural Park of the Mountain of Montserrat under the control of the Patronat.

An impressive all-embracing aerial view.

Montserrat

The monastery is usually peaceful in the morning, but by midday crowds of visitors have begun to arrive.

THE «MORENETA»

History testifies that just after the current image of Saint Mary –Our Lady– was put in place in the Romanesque church, the number of the faithful and the fame of the Monastery grew progressively. At the beginning of the thirteenth century, James I was already talking of the small church of Montserrat as a place «which God embellishes and illustrates with continuous miracles». Precisely during those years, the Confraria (brotherhood) of devotees of Our Lady of Montserrat was established. This institution has, over the centuries, had many members who have spiritually adhered to the monastic community and have trusted to its prayer.

The «Moreneta» (dark woman), commonly so called because of the dark colour of her face, is a Romanesque wooden sculpture dating from the end of the twelfth or beginning of the thirteenth century. Restoration work was required on many subsequent occasions and particularly after the Napoleonic Wars of the nineteenth century. The image, a work of serene austere beauty, possibly owes its colour to the slow change in the varnish (by a process of oxidation) on the face and hands caused by the passage of time and the effect of candle smoke and lamps burnt over many years in the small Romanesque church. However, it cannot be ruled out that from the very beginning the Holy Image was meant to represent the wife in the book of the Song of Songs, who is dark and beautiful according to the biblical story and the sung liturgy of the Church.

Our Lady is crowned with a diadem and wears

The Gothic cloister (built by Julio Segundo in 1479), by Jaume Alfons i Pere Basset.

a headdress of many colours and a golden robe and cloak; she is sitting in a hieratic position and holds a ball in her right hand. The Child is sitting on her lap. He is crowned and clothed in a similar fashion and making a sign of blessing with His right hand while holding a pine cone in His left. The sculpture was moved from the Romanesque church to its current site in 1599. In 1881 she was crowned in accordance with canon law and proclaimed patron of the dioceses in Catalonia and in 1947 was placed upon her current throne.

This image of the Mother of Jesus has grown in importance over the course of the years and is the expression of a spiritual presence on Montserrat which makes her both venerable and attractive. The image represents one of central tenets of the Christian faith: the mystery of

Close-up of a capital in the Gothic cloister.

Montserrat

The Escolanía (choir), documented as far back as the 13th century.

the Incarnation, of the Son of God made man in Jesus of Nazareth. Mary, with her son in her arms, reveals the love of God for man, to whom Jesus offers life and immortality (symbolised by the pine cone) through the Easter mystery of his death and resurrection, which is at the centre of Christianity. The mystery of the Incarnation, which culminates at Easter, sustains the universe created by God (symbolised by the orb which Saint Mary holds in her hands).

THE CHOIR

There is already documentary evidence of the existence of the Montserrat Choir at the end of the thirteenth century. The Choir is a religious and musical institution made up of young boys. Whatever the date it started, it can be consi-

dered now as the oldest conservatoire in Europe. It probably originated from one of the «schools of psalm and song» which existed at the end of the twelfth century in the cathedrals and other churches in Catalonia, and has continued through to our times, reaching the high level of quality for which it is world famous. Over the centuries, the Choir has produced a number of choir-masters, organists and instrumentalists for the Church and has trained notable teachers and composers, particularly during the seventeenth and eighteenth centuries.

The Shrine has many features, of which the Choir is one of the most popular and charming, as demonstrated by the great number of visitors and pilgrims who attend the singing of the Salve Regina at midday. There are currently fifty choirboys, who receive an introduction to

Montserrat

Portal of the old Romanesque church (12th century).

Front of the basilica, with the sculptures by the Vallmitjana brothers.

Image of the atrium, with the tomb of John of Aragon in the foreground.

Montserrat

Presbytery and choir.   Interior of the basilica.

music in accordance with the ancient tradition of Montserrat. As well as voice training, solfeggio, polyphonic singing and gregorian chant, the boys receive a social, literary and scientific education and must also study a specific musical instrument, while the most gifted are instructed in the techniques of composing music. The choirboys often take part in the prayers of the Shrine with the community of monks and continue, through their musical offering, the tradition of centuries.

THE BASILICA

The uneven land on which the Shrine of Montserrat is built means that its construction is entirely irregular in shape. The group of buildings –built, destroyed and then recon-

structed over the course of the years– consists of two large sections: the Basilica with monastic outbuildings and the buildings for accommodating and providing services for pilgrims and tourists. In artistic terms, the more interesting part by far is the Basilica and outbuildings.

The Atrium

At the end of the upper squares, the most notable feature is the robust shape of the west end of the Monastery with its tower that was constructed after the 1936–39 civil war. This entire architectural group reveals the character of its architect, Francesc Folguera. The three large balconies at the top are decorated with reliefs which, apart from the lower panels that form the lower part of the frame of the door to the central balcony, are the work of the sculptor Joan Rebull.

Montserrat

Staircase to the *Camerin*, with reliefs by Enric Monjo.

series of scratch-work and sculptures of saints or kings connected with Montserrat in its combined role of Benedictine Monastery and Marian Shrine. Images which stand out are those of St. John the Baptist and Saint Joseph sculpted by Josep Clarà. In this atrium is the baptistry with its door which has a representation of the cycle of Church sacraments according to the catechism beginning with baptism.

The Church

Abbot Bartomeu Garriga, as we have already seen, was responsible for the building of the Basilica of Montserrat in the sixteenth century. The works were carried out under the direction

Image of Our Lady.

In the lower part, below the arches, there are two sixteenth century tombs, the porch of the old Romanesque church (twelfth century) and a statue of Saint Benedict in wrought iron by Domènec Fita. Leaning against this façade are two wings from the Gothic cloister which was built in 1376 by the masters of Barcelona, Jaume Alfons and Pere Basset, on the orders of the abbot in commendam (who held the office in the absence of a regular incumbent and did not reside at Montserrat) of the time, Giuliano della Rovere, who was to be the future Pope Julius II, and whose shield decorates this lithe late-Gothic building.

The atrium that provides access to the church is from the eighteenth century, although it did undergo some alterations in the middle of the twentieth century. Of particular note are the

Throne of Our Lady.

Montserrat

*Pilgrims take an active part in all religious
celebrations at Montserrat.*

of Miquel Sastre and took thirty-two years to complete because of the magnitude of the project and the natural difficulties presented by the site. It was consecrated on 2 February 1592 and opened to the faithful. Leo XIII raised it to the status of basilica in 1881. The original plateresque façade was replaced between 1900 and 1901 by the current façade, which is the work of Francesc de P. Villar with sculptures by the brothers Venanci and Agàpit Vallmitjana.

The central aisle is 68.32 metres long, 21.5 wide and 33.33 high. In spite of the period when it was built, it is covered with very rounded Gothic arches which are firmly supported by the walls which separate the six side chapels. Together, they constitute an unusual building amongst the monuments of Catalonia and mark the transition from the Gothic to Renaissance. The interior of the church was restored with somewhat eclectic decoration following the destruction by Napoleon's armies. A programme of works was carried out between 1992 and 1996 to return the exterior to its original Renaissance design, which was lost due

to various additions. The interior also underwent some restoration so that more light could enter through the reopening of the side windows and the octagonal dome to offset the shady colour the building had acquired over the course of time. All of this work was overseen by the architect Arcadi Pla.

Along the length of the central aisle are numerous votive lamps of extraordinary gold-work, with some pieces of exceptional beauty. These lamps were offered by the cities and districts of Catalonia and by various groups and organisations. The statues of the prophets Ezekiel, Jeremiah, Isaiah and Daniel by Josep Llimona stand out amongst the central abutments. All four prophets speak about the arrival of the Messiah in their books and so occupy an important place in the Marian Basilica.

The most remarkable part of the interior is the Presbytery surrounded by three rows of neo-Gothic choir-stalls for the community of monks. The walls are decorated with a series of paintings by Joan Llimona, Baixeres, Graner and Riquer, which form a unique collection of

Modernista *Catalan paintings on a religious theme. In the centre, placed on some green marble steps, is the high altar –a block of stone weighing 8,000 kilos taken from the mountain itself– which has an antependium with enamels by Montserrat Mainar. Above the altar, hanging from the baldachin canopy, there is an ivory Christ figure, attributed to Ghiberti (sixteenth century), nailed to a cross decorated with Easter stories from the middle of the twentieth century. To the right of the aisle is the chapel of the Holy Sacrament, which underwent changes in 1977 with sculptures by Subirachs and work by the Capdevila goldsmiths. Also of note are the chapels of Mary Immaculate (on the right-hand side), Sant Martí and Sant Josep de Calassanç in the* Modernista *style and of Saint Benedict with a painting by Montserrat Gudiol (on the left-hand side).*

The Niche

The wide marble staircase which leads to the Niche, located at the back of the church, opens out into a carved alabaster doorway by Enric Monjo with Marian stories and flanked by two candelabra that are also made of alabaster by Rafael Solanich. The interior of the stairway is decorated with beautifully-made mosaics designed by Fr. Benet Martínez, one of the monks of Montserrat. The two antechambers to the throne of the Holy Image contain paintings by Josep Obiols. Two pairs of beaten silver doors lead to the small throne room, visible from the central aisle. The dome and walls of the throne room are decorated with golden mosaics designed by Obiols, which show Our Lady of Montserrat being proclaimed patron saint of Catalonia and other Marian scenes. There are nine worked silver lamps, representing the eight Catalan dioceses and the Community of Montserrat, around the room. Reliefs by Joaquim Ros representing the Nativity and the Visitation of Mary flank the throne. Above the

The Camerin, built with the assistance of Gaudí .

Montserrat

Image there are reproductions of the crown, sceptre and lily offered by the people of Catalonia to Our Lady (the originals are kept in the museum).

The back part of this room leads to the circular niche built between 1876 and 1884 by Villar i Carmona in a pre-Modernista style with Gothic and Romanesque features. The famous architect Gaudí played an important role in the direction of this work. The vault is decorated with frescos by Joan Llimona, which show the pilgrims of Montserrat being received by Saint Mary.

The exit from the niche is via the Path of the Ave Maria, where pilgrims leave the candles they offer to Our Lady as an act of thanks or in remembrance of the prayer they have said at the Shrine. The route is decorated by a series of pieces

of majolica which have Marian invocations on them. A piece of sculpture by Apel.les Fenosa evokes the angel of the Annunciation to Mary.

The New Sacristy

The new Sacristy was built by the architect Francesc Folguera and consists of a vestibule, a spacious room with cupboards and a small apse. In the vestibule there is the tomb and statue in bronze by Joaquim Ros of the Venerable Fr. Josep de Sant Benet, a monk who died in 1723 and who is remembered for his holiness. The entire vault is decorated in a distinctly idealistic style with biblical stories of the Eucharist and scenes of Christmas, Easter and Pentecost by Josep Obiols. The mahogany cupboards along the side walls have marquetry panels –also designed by Josep Obiols– which show

The new sacristy, with paintings and marquetry by Josep Obiols.

saints and other figures linked to Montserrat. The ensemble is extremely beautiful and has especially well-balanced lines.

The Crypt

A small staircase located in the right-hand side of the Presbytery, at the side of the niche chamber itself, leads down to the Crypt. This sober harmonious barrel-vaulted room was opened in 1951 and designed as the burial place for Abbot Antoni M. Marcet and the twenty-three monks who gave their lives to Christ in the civil war of 1936–39.

The tombs are placed in two vaults opened in the wall; each has a Carrara marble gravestone engraved with details of the remains contained in the vault. At the back of the room there is a memorial stone to those monks whose remains could not be found. The body of Abbot Marcet lies in a sarcophagus designed by Joan Rebull in the centre of the room behind the altar.

In the side walls are also to be found the tombs and gravestones of Cardinal Anselm M. Albareda, the Abbots Gregori Sunyol, Aureli M. Escarré, Gabriel M. Brasó and Pere Celestí Gusi, all the monks of Montserrat, of Fr. Bernardo López, who was abbot at the Monastery of Our Lady of Montserrat in Manila, and of Bishop Antoni Urbss of Latvia together with his secretary, both of whom died in exile at the Monastery.

The Upper Choir

The Upper Choir, which until 1934 was the only one in the Basilica, is supported by Gothic arches above the chancel of the Church. The

Montserrat

The Annunciation, *a 16th-century panel.*

most notable feature is the group of neoclassical walnut choir-stalls which replaced the Renaissance choir-stalls carved by Cristóbal de Salamanca in the sixteenth century and burnt during the Napoleonic Wars (apart from a few panels and columns which still remain). The current choir-stalls –a gift to the Monastery from Ferdinand VII– were designed in 1824 by Antoni Cellés, who was the first director of the architecture class at the School of the Noble Arts of the Llotja in Barcelona.

The large nineteenth century polychromatic rose representing the coronation and glorification of Mary is also worthy of note.

THE MONASTERY

The Community of Monks

The current Montserrat community, consisting of some eighty monks, is dedicated, as in times gone by, to a life of prayer, work and hospitality for the thousands upon thousands of pilgrims who visit the Shrine. In accordance with the spirit of the Rule of Saint Benedict (a spiritual way of life written in the sixth century but which is sufficiently adaptable to every epoch and every socio-cultural situation), the monks try to live a life of praise and intercession in adoring silence, using the depth of their experience of God and their knowledge of the most profound longings of the human soul in order better to serve men and women everywhere.

Benedictine monasticism is particularly coenobitic (communitarian), and so the monk becomes a brother amongst brothers who help him on his path towards God and enable him to live a life of fraternal love as described in the Gospels.

Prayer

The monks have always tried to combine solitude with hospitality, two concepts which would appear to be mutually exclusive but which in fact are not. The tension between the two has been fruitful over the years for the monks themselves, the Church and for society. The secular history of the community of Montserrat is eloquent proof of this. Solitude enables the individual to find the light of the Word of God; thus the person gradually moves towards self-acceptance, peace and inner harmony. This occurs above all during the passionate search for God through the liturgy and private prayer.

The liturgy marks the daily rhythm for the monastic day, marking both its beginning and end. The monks come together five times a day to celebrate divine service or the Liturgy of the Hours. In addition to this, there is the celebration of the Eucharist, which is the central event in the day of the Monastery and Shrine. Many pilgrims take part in the monks' liturgy, particularly in the Eucharist and the main hours of divine service.

The monks also set part of the day aside for private prayer and for reading the Word of God or other spiritual works. The ideal situation, as given both by the New Testament and by the Benedictine Rule, is for prayer to God to be as continuous as possible.

Hospitality
The life of the monks in terms of humanity and faith is no different to the basic experience of all men and women because, when all is told, we all live with the same problems around us: problems regarding love, solitude, personal harmony, solidarity, work, use of material goods... and, sometimes, wearied or even weak faith.
The life of faith leads the monk to discover the presence of Christ in another, whoever he or she may be. This means the monk must welcome

him or her in a sincere and friendly manner and must feel himself to be the brother of all people.

Work
This openness to solidarity and communion with all manifests itself at Montserrat through various pastoral activities: services at the Basilica, welcoming of groups, retreats and conferences, the provision of lodgings (allowing individuals or groups to spend a few days of reflection and prayer following the rhythm of the monastic community at its most important moments), etc.
In addition to this pastoral work, the monastic chores include the humble tasks required to

Saint Benet, *by Josep Clarà.*

Montserrat

Chapterhouse.

ensure the good running of the Monastery and the Shrine and some craft work. There are also monks involved in scientific research in various fields including history, theology, translation, biblical studies, liturgy and philosophy.

The Monastery has a notable publications service, which publishes numerous books and magazines on science or for circulation on specifically religious as well as cultural themes. The service also puts together records and audiovisual material. Indeed, Montserrat occupies an important position as one of the principal centres of Catalan culture.

Shaped as it is by its uninterrupted history in this place, the community today dedicates itself to the constant search for renewed faith in accordance with the demands of the Church and with its loyalty to the men and women of

our times, in its own monastic tradition, in order to continue its service to mankind and especially to the Christians of the country with which it has always been so closely linked.

The Chapter House

This sober, beautifully decorated square-shaped room is the meeting place for the monastic community for important events. The more informal daily meetings are held elsewhere. The Monastery lives as a family and shares both its spiritual as well as material goods, in an attempt to live a Christian life to the full in accordance with the evangelical spirit contained in the Rule of Saint Benedict and under the guidance of an abbot. This fraternal communion involves an element of dialogue, of communication, so that each member of the community is jointly responsible for the running of the Monastery and helps the abbot in determining the courses of action to be taken.

This room is used for these serious moments of deliberation, judgment and decision-making at a community level and also for the monastic conferences which the abbot addresses to the community from time to time.

Near the Chapter House is the Room of the Sign, watched over by a bronze statue of Saint Benedict by Josep Clarà. A sepulchral monument to Abbot Oliba by Enric Monjo and a statue of Abbot Garsias de Cisneros by Francesc Juventeny can be found in this room.

The Neo-Romanesque Cloister

The Cloister, constructed in the interior of the Monastery and which connects various out-

buildings, was built by Puig i Cadafalch in 1925 in a «Romanesque» style using an unusual combination of stone, brick and wood. The aim of its particularly beautiful lines is to reflect the architectural shapes from the primitive period of the Monastery of Santa Maria.

It is formed by two storeys of brick arches supported by stone columns. All along the walls there is a sizable collection of archeological pieces and gravestones, important for their historical and artistic merit, dating from the tenth to the eighteenth century. The lower floor has a small pavilion with a fountain in the centre, which evokes the great monastic cloisters of Catalonia, and connects to the garden. The wealth of different types of trees and plants in the garden attracts birds, and their singing

Neo-Romanesque cloister, built by Josep Puig i Cadafalch in 1925.

Montserrat

The refectory, built in the 17th century and reformed in 1925.

combined with the sound of the fountain produces a tranquil setting for reflection and peace.

The Refectory

Meals are an important part of fraternal life; the Bible itself emphasises their spiritual nature and teaches that God is present in the communion amongst those eating. Monastic rules therefore give an almost liturgical air to meals, which begin and end in prayer and are conducted in silence. The aim is to feed not only the body but also the spirit through reading which accompanies the meal. The consequence is that refectories in monasteries have a special architectural feel.

The refectory at Montserrat is large and very light and dates from the seventeenth century with some alterations made in 1925 by Puig i Cadafalch. On one side it overlooks the side of the rock itself and on the other, large windows give an excellent view of the mountain. At the presiding end, there is a side apse covered in mosaics showing the Christ in Majesty, inspired by wall paintings in the Pyrenees. At the opposite end, there is a triptych painted in cheerful colours by Josep Obiols, which shows a scene from the life of Saint Benedict. In the centre, there is a stone throne for the reader.

The Library

The library at Montserrat is valuable both for the quality and quantity of its collection of books. There are some 250,000 volumes, including approximately 400 incunabula and 2,000 manuscripts. The collection also holds

Library: central room with, in the background, a fresco by Sert.

the oldest known example of written Catalan from the end of the twelfth or early thirteenth century.

There is documentary evidence of the library at Montserrat as early as the eleventh century. The collection grew over the years but the Napoleonic Wars, responsible for so much destruction on the mountain, caused the disappearance or dispersal of a large number of its books and archives. Apart from a few pieces which were saved, the current stock was started during the period of reconstruction, particularly during the abbacy of Fr. Antoni M. Marcet. The library has subsequently been enriched by many new additions.

Amongst the manuscripts is the famous fourteenth century Llibre Vermell *(Red Book)* with miniatures from the Montserrat Scriptorium.

A corner of the monastery garden.

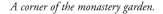

Montserrat

Resurrection of the Mysteries of the Rosary, a fine work by Gaudí and Llimona.

Interior of the Holy Cave, where, according to popular legend, the image of the Virgin was found.

This book is a veritable encyclopedia to medieval Montserrat, its importance being due in part to the collection of the oldest songs and dances in Europe from the pilgrims to the Shrine.

THE VIA CRUCIS

The Way of the Cross begins a little beyond the Plaça Abat Oliba behind the Font del Portal (the Fountain of the Portal) and continues on to the Chapel of Our Lady of Sorrows, close to the Sant Miquel path. The route is gentle and beautifully shaded and is one of the prettiest places in the area, offering a pleasant panorama of the Shrine.

Fourteen monuments corresponding to the

Stations of the Cross were erected between 1904 and 1919 but were completely destroyed in the 1936 war. Some new Stations have been set up using sculptures by Margarida Sans Jordi and Francesc Juventeny; the remaining Stations will be by Domènec Fita using a particularly stylised design.

LA SANTA COVA

The path which leads to the Santa Cova (Holy Cave) starts near the cable car and continues for about one and a half kilometres along a route established in the seventeenth century. Financial support from the faithful contributed to the fifteen sculptural groups corresponding to the fifteen Mysteries of the Rosary

set up along the route. Gaudí, Puig i Cadafalch, Josep Llimona, the Vallmitjana brothers and others all worked on these pieces of sculpture. Almost hanging from the rock at the end of the route is the Chapel where legend has it that the Image of Our Lady of Montserrat was found. The current building is by and large the same as the seventeenth century building which was rebuilt twice, firstly because of the damage suffered in the Napoleonic Wars in 1811 and later after damage caused by the fire in 1994 and the collapse of the dome in September 1995.

There are some outbuildings used as a dwelling by the monk who welcomes pilgrims there and a charming small cloister. The simple small chapel, built to the design of a Greek cross and dome, backs onto a grotto in the mountain, where there is a stylised reproduction of the authentic Image in the Basilica. The entire place is peaceful and solitary.

SANTA CECÍLIA

The Monastery of Santa Cecília is located some four kilometres from Montserrat, at the side of the road which leads to Can Maçana, near a popular restaurant.

The simple bare church is basically the same as that constructed in the tenth century and is one of the purest examples of Romanesque primitive Catalan art. Its three apses, decorated with blind arcades of Lombardy arches, correspond to each of the three interior aisles with hammered stone walls that were originally white. This construction fits beautifully into the landscape, producing an attractive combination.

The Monastery was founded between 942 and 945 by Abbot Cesari. The community has never been particularly large and in 1539 it was finally linked to Montserrat, which now uses the monastic building as a reception site.

The Chapel of Sant Iscle is cited in documents going back as far of the 9th century.

Apse of the old Monastery of Santa Cecilia, with 10th-century church.

Montserrat

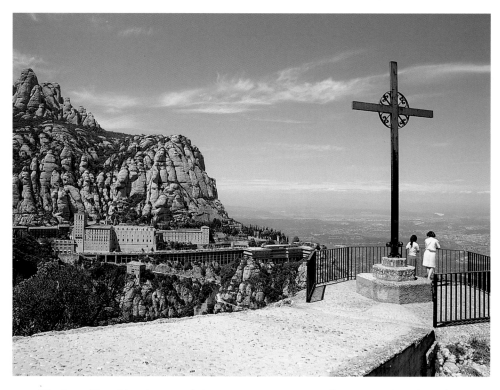

The Cross of Sant Miquel commands fine views of the magnificent landscape.

The Sant Joan funicular railway.

Surrounding the buildings there is a landscaped grove which offers a wide panorama from the Pyrenees, snow-covered in winter, all the way to Mediterranean. A good way to finish the visit to Santa Cecília is with a walk across the mountain along strange narrow paths to the ruins of the former hermitages of Santa Anna, Sant Salvador, Sant Benet, the Holy Trinity, etc., all of which are lovingly evocative of history and legend.

THE HERMITAGE OF SANT MIQUEL

Although there is documentary evidence of the hermitage going back to the tenth century, the current building is of much later

The Hermitage of Sant Miquel watches over the mountain from the old Collbató road.

Montserrat

44

Montserrat

Entrance to the museum.

construction. Many pilgrims of all social classes visit this site, following the wide path which leaves Plaça Abat Oliba and initially runs along the ancient Collbató way, the most important itinerary of medieval Montserrat. A path goes off to the left approximately a hundred metres from the chapel and leads to a belvedere on top of a precipice over two hundred metres high, where there is a magnificent view of the Llobregat valley below with the Pyrenees in the background.

This route is one of the easiest and most attractive in the area and can be extended by a visit, by funicular or on foot, to the hermitages of Sant Joan and Sant Jeroni, where there is another marvellous high view of Montserrat and a large part of Catalonia.

THE MUSEUM

In 1811 with the Napoleonic Wars, Montserrat lost almost all of its artistic heritage, as we have already seen with the library. In spite of this, a valuable collection of works of art, mostly donated, has been built up since the restoration in 1844. Most of these works are on show in the Museum located below the upper square of the Shrine. This same space, designed by Josep Puig i Cadafalch in 1929, is particularly unusual from an architectural point of view because of the technique used to support the square and the two lower floors.

The Museum is divided into various sections: archeology of the Bible lands, gold-work in the Shrine's Sacristy, paintings by old masters and

Montserrat

Archaeology of the Biblical East, with objects from Mesopotamia, Egypt, Cyprus and the Holy Land.

Vases with animal shapes.

Montserrat

evidence of the different periods of Mesopotamian history.

From Egypt, there is a collection of ancient funerary objects including a mummy of a twenty-five year old woman from the late period, two sarcophagi, two Canopic vases, statuettes and amulets.

The collection of objects from Palestine includes ceramics from a number of biblical epochs, some dating from 4000 BC; coins, statues of Greek and Caananite gods, Roman and Byzantine glasses, an extensive collection of lamps, etc. The collection of Cypriot ceramics is also interesting, with the earliest pieces dating from the twentieth century BC.

Masks of the mummy in the Egypt room.

the extraordinary collection of Catalan paintings and sculptures from the nineteenth and twentieth centuries.

Archeology of the Bible Lands

The archeology of the Bible lands is represented by an important collection of pieces connected to countries in the Bible (Mesopotamia, Egypt, Cyprus and Palestine). The monk Bonaventura Ubach (who died in 1960) gathered these pieces together and began studies of the Bible at Montserrat, which were continued by his followers. In addition to the most important pieces which are on permanent display, the Museum has an alternating show for visitors and scholars of its reserve.

Important pieces from Mesopotamia are the numerous cuneiform tablets in Akkadian, Hittite and Sumerian dating from 3400 BC to 600 BC. There is also a sizeable collection of stone cylinders, with their seals, which provide

Montserrat

Archaeology of the Biblical East.
18th-century torah.

Torah and pectoral crosses, necklaces and amulets.

Montserrat

49

Gold-work

Gold-work is represented in the Montserrat Museum by a collection of accessories to the liturgy (chalices, patens, cruets, crowns, monstrances, pectoral crosses, etc.) from the fifteenth to the twentieth century, which show the development in techniques and artistic styles. The richly decorated crown and sceptre offered by the Catalans to Our Lady in 1881 when she was proclaimed patron saint of Catalonia are of special importance. There are also the Baroque cruets and chalice of enamelled gold given to Montserrat by Emperor Ferdinand III of Austria in thanks for his victory over Gustavus Adolphus of Italy and the rock crystal reliquary offered to Our Lady in 1605 by the duke of Mantua and Montferrat, Vincenzo de Gonzaga.

Paintings by Old Masters

This important collection contains old masters from he thirteenth to the eighteenth century including works by Berruguete, Morales, el Greco, Bonfigli, A. de Salerno, Marco Pino, Caravaggio, Luca Giordano and Tiepolo. A large number of these paintings were acquired in Italy between 1914 and 1920 during the time of Abbot Antoni M. Marcet. Catalan and Castilian painting is represented by canvasses from the fifteenth and sixteenth centuries.

Modern Painting and Sculpture

The modern painting and sculpture collection contains a representative selection of work by Catalan artists who were working between the middle of the nineteenth and the middle of the twentieth centuries. The initial core, which went on show in 1982, consists of works from the Josep Sala i Ardiz Collection by artists such as Martí Alsina, Vayreda, Gimeno, Rusiñol, Casas, Nonell, Mir, Anglada Camarasa, Picasso and Dalí. Some years later the Xavier Busquets Collection of French Impressionist paintings was added, with works by Monet, Sisley, Degas, Pissarro, Rouault and Poliakoff.

Objects in precious metal from the 15th to the 20th centuries.

Entrance to the room devoted to painting from the 13th to the 18th centuries.
Room in the modern painting and sculpture section.

Montserrat

51

Saint Jerome, *by Caravaggio (1573-1610).*

Madonnina, *by Mateo de Giovanni (1435-1495).*

Montserrat

53

Madeleine. Absinthe, *by Ramon Casas (1865-1932).*

The Old Fisherman, *by Pablo Picasso (1881-1973).*

Bread and Grapes, *by Salvador Dalí (1901-1989).*

Poor boy, *by Isidre Nonell (1873-1911).*

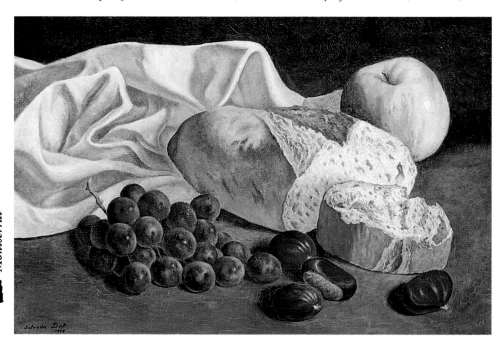

Montserrat

The Path to the Cave, *by Joaquim Mir*
(1873-1940).

Works by other artists such as Singer Sargent, Sorolla, Julio Romero de Torres and Zuloaga complete this section of the museum. The artists represented mean that the Museum of Montserrat has one of the best collections of Catalan Modernista *and French Impressionist painting in Catalonia.*

«Nigra sum»: *Iconography of Saint Mary of Montserrat*

The Museum also has a permanent exhibition on the history of the Image of Our Lady of Montserrat to help pilgrims and visitors understand the historical evolution of the Image of Saint Mary that is venerated at Montserrat.

This exhibition is entitled Nigra sum meaning «I am a black woman» in reference to the text in the book of the Song of Songs 1, 5 which says «I am black, but comely», words which perfectly suit the Image of Our Lady of Montserrat in the physical sense as well as in the symbolic or theological sense referred to above. The exhibition shows the developments in the rich iconography over the course of various epochs, from the twelfth century to 1947 when the Image was installed on the throne in the Niche. There are pieces of sculpture, paintings (Joan A. Ricci, c.1639; Olga Sacharoff, 1947, and others), drawings, engravings (some from 1499), medals, etc.

Our Lady of Montserrat, *by Juan A. Ricci (1600-1681).*

At night, Montserrat is embraced once more by a serene silence.

THE POPULAR ASPECT OF MONTSERRAT

Montserrat has many features, one of which is its extraordinary popularity. Many Catalans make a customary annual visit, either individually or with their family. There are frequent weddings, birthdays, public festivals and other similar events. Some families or groups spend Easter in its characteristic setting or they come for a few days of relaxation and brotherhood during the summer holidays. Some parishes organise pilgrimages, during which time Montserrat takes on a festive air and offers a renewal of Christian life according to a pastoral plan proposed each year by the Shrine. Many cultural and religious groups include a visit to the Shrine as part of their activities and leave flags, emblems or other offerings as evidence of their stay. It is frequently even the setting for cultural events or popular festivals. On certain occasions, people express their joy by dancing the sardana, the traditional dance of Catalonia. However, these events have been influenced by the social changes that are characteristic of our age, taking on new forms. Tourism has had a particularly strong influence on the appearance of Montserrat in recent years, particularly in spring and summer when large groups of visitors effectively invade the Shrine.

Montserrat is a natural phenomenon which, in addition to its principal religious function, has become a cultural centre, a popular place for excursions and tourist visits and an attractive location for many climbers, all facilitated by easy means of transport. All of this contributes to increasing the interest which this holy, beautiful mountain has always aroused far and wide throughout Catalonia.

The squares of the Sanctuary bear witness to the passing of the centuries and of many, many generations of people.

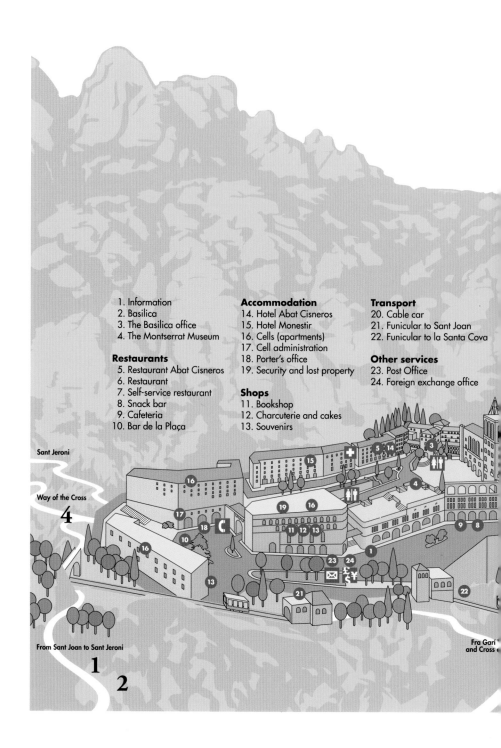

1. Information
2. Basilica
3. The Basilica office
4. The Montserrat Museum

Restaurants
5. Restaurant Abat Cisneros
6. Restaurant
7. Self-service restaurant
8. Snack bar
9. Cafeteria
10. Bar de la Plaça

Accommodation
14. Hotel Abat Cisneros
15. Hotel Monestir
16. Cells (apartments)
17. Cell administration
18. Porter's office
19. Security and lost property

Shops
11. Bookshop
12. Charcuterie and cakes
13. Souvenirs

Transport
20. Cable car
21. Funicular to Sant Joan
22. Funicular to la Santa Cova

Other services
23. Post Office
24. Foreign exchange office

Sant Jeroni

Way of the Cross

From Sant Joan to Sant Jeroni

Fra Garí
and Cross

Montserrat

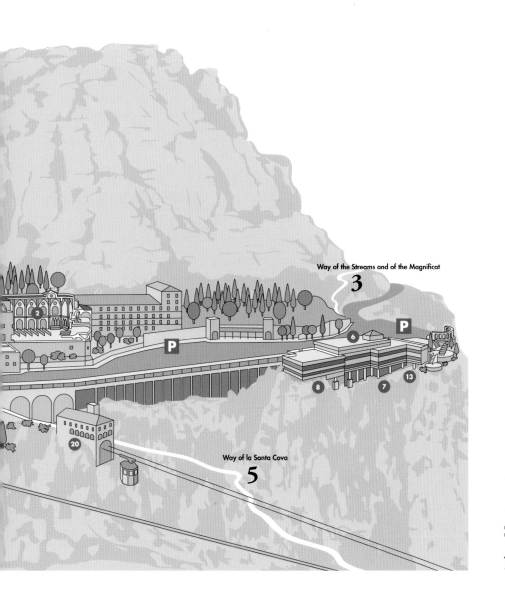

Way of the Streams and of the Magnificat

3

Way of la Santa Cova

5

Montserrat

1. Hermitage of Sant Joan

This route takes us to visit one of the most easily accessible of the thirteen hermitages on Mount Montserrat, that of Sant Joan. Take the Sant Joan funicular railway, enjoying from the upper station fine views of the monastery and sanctuary. A pleasant path leads from the station to the hermitage, a walk of around twenty minutes. On the right, hanging from the rock, is the Hermitage of Sant Onofre. Back at the Sant Joan funicular railway station, the same path leads to the Hermitage of Sant Jeroni.

2. Hermitage of Sant Jeroni

We can reach the Hermitage of Sant Jeroni by a path from the Sant Joan funicular railway station, a walk taking around one and a half hours, or by taking the Sant Jeroni cablecar (currently out of service). In any case, this is one of the most beautiful excursions in the Montserrat Natural Park, culminating at the Peak of Sant Jeroni, the highest point on the mountain (1,236 metres). At the Sant Joan funicular railway station, we take the path skirting the peak to enter the leafy wood. Along the way, we can enjoy magnificent panoramic views of, on the opposite side of the river valley, from right to left, the hermitages of Sant Dimes, La Santa Creu, la Santíssima Trinitat and Sant Benet. We finally reach the Hermitage of Sant Jeroni, beside which is a staircase leading up to the peak of the same name. Those beginning or terminating the excursion at the lower station of the Sant Jeroni cablecar station are recommended the visit to the Church and Monastery of Santa Cecília (500 metres), which stands beside a restaurant.

3. Els Degotalls and El Magníficat

This excursion, taking around 45 minutes to complete, starts out on the road near the restaurant and car park area. Before starting out along the path, we can enjoy a magnificent panoramic view of the Llobregat River Valley from the terraces of the restaurants. On a clear day, we can see as far as Mount Tibidabo and the Mediterranean Sea to the east and the Pyrenees to the north. Just a few metres along the road we find, on our left, the path leading to Els Degotalls, a rock formation from which water once flowed. Along this walk, some twenty minutes in duration, we can enjoy splendid views over the Bages district and the Pyrenees, coming across various monuments referring to the cultural life and folklore of Catalonia. The path also forms the starting-point for the visit to El Magníficat, decorated with fine tiles representing different dedications to the Virgin Mary.

4. Stations of the Cross and the Path to the Hermitage of Sant Miquel

The Via Crucis begins in Plaça del Abad Molina, behind the sculpture of the Fountain of El Portal, and ends at the Chapel of La Dolorosa, where we can take the Path to the Hermitage of Sant Miquel to return to our point of origin. These two paths, with a duration of around 20 and 45 minutes respectively, form one of the most beautiful walks in the area, offering fine views of the sanctuary in the case of the first and of the magnificent surrounding landscape in the case of the second. The fourteen stations of the Via Crucis found along the first walk were built between 1909 and 1914, though they were completely destroyed in 1936, soon after the outbreak of the Spanish Civil War. The present sculptures are by Margarida Sans Jordi, Francesc Juventeny and Domènec Fita. Towards the end of the path is the Chapel of La Verge de Soledat (1910). Near the fourteenth station, we join up with the Path to the Hermitage of Sant

Miquel, the most important of medieval Montserrat. The Hermitage of Sant Miquel and the viewpoint known as the Mirador de Fra Garí are the main points of interest along this route. The viewpoint, situated around 100 metres from the hermitage, stands at the top of a precipice over 200 metres in height, and commands magnificent panoramic views of the Llobregat Valley and the Pyrenees. Beside the viewpoint is an iron cross evoking those which once flanked the path to Montserrat.

5. Path to the Holy Cave

The path leading to the Holy Cave starts out from Plaça de la Santa Creu, beside the cable car station. Created in the 17th century, the path follows a route around one and a half kilometres in length. An alternative is to take the funicular railway to the Holy Cave, which leaves us halfway along the path. This traditional path is adorned by fifteen sculptural groups depicting the Mysteries of the Rosary. All these sculptures date to the late-19th and early-20th centuries and were paid for by popular subscription. They are by various artists, including such renowned names as Gaudí, Puig i Cadafalch, Llimona and the Vallmitjana brothers. At the end of the path, almost hanging from the rock, is the cave chapel where, according to popular legend, the image of the Virgin of Montserrat was found.

Montserrat

CONTENTS

A SURPRISING WORLD 4
THE MONASTERY IS BORN 7
HISTORICAL BACKGROUND 9
A LAND OF FANTASY:
THE NATURAL PARK 20
THE «MORENETA» 24
THE CHOIR 26
THE BASILICA..28
THE MONASTERY.....................................36
THE VIA CRUCIS......................................42
LA SANTA COVA 42
SANTA CECÍLIA..43
THE HERMITAGE OF SANT MIQUEL 44
THE MUSEUM...46
THE POPULAR ASPECT OF
MONTSERRAT...58
ITINERARIES 62

Montserrat